LIFE AND ADVENTURES

OF

ROBERT,

THE

HERMIT OF MASSACHUSETTS,

Who Has Lived 14 Years in a Cave, Secluded from Human Society.

COMPRISING,

An account of his Birth, Parentage, Sufferings, and
providential escape from unjust and cruel Bondage
in early life--and his reasons for becoming
a Recluse.
Taken from his own mouth, and published for his benefit.

BY

ROBERT VOORHIS

PRINTED FOR

HENRY TRUMBULL

ROBERT THE HERMIT.

LIFE AND ADVENTURES
OF
ROBERT THE HERMIT.

IT is a fact well known to almost every inhabitant of Rhode Island, that on the summit of a hill, a few rods east of Seekonk river, (within the State of Massachusetts) and about two miles from Providence Bridge, has dwelt for many years, a solitary HERMIT, bearing the name of ROBERT--and, although familiarly known to many of the inhabitants of Providence, and its vicinity, for his peaceable and agreeable disposition, yet, his history, as regards his birth, the cause of his seclusion, &c. has until very recently remained a profound secret! having carefully avoided answering any questions relative thereto, of hundreds, who, prompted by curiosity, have been from time to time induced to visit his cave, or cell--and although very peaceable and civil in his deportment, he has (with the exception of his occasional excursions to Providence, and the adjacent villages, to obtain food and necessaries) remained almost impervious in his retreat.

Many and various have been the conjectures. The most curious and inquisitive of the Rhode Islanders, (in the, neighborhood of whose State he lives,) respecting this "strange and mysterious being," and while some few have unjustly harboured an opinion that he had perpetrated crimes of a heniousnature for which he was doing penance--others, have avowed in opposition to this, that his whole deportment was so perfectly calm, and his countenance so serene, that it was impossible that so fair a tenant could harbour a soul of darkness and criminality.

The first information which the writer ever received of this extraordinary character was through the medium of one of the Providence prints, containing some well written remarks relating to him, and which we have thought proper here to republish in confirmation of the fact stated, that, until very recently "Robert the Hermit" has uniformly refused to gratify the curiosity of any of his visitors, as regarded his nativity, history, &c.

From the Literary Cadet of June 1826.

"Beneath a mountain's brow, the most remote
And inaccessible by Shepherds trod,
In a deep cave, dug by no mortals hands
An Hermit lived,--a melancholy man
Who was the wonder of our wand'ring swains:
Austere and lonely--cruel to himself
They did report him--the cold earth his bed,
Water his drink, his food the Shepherd's alms.
I went to see him, and my heart was touched
With reverence and pity. Mild he spake,
And entering on discourse, such stories told,
As made me oft re-visit his sad cell."

Homes' Douglas.

"On the declivity of a hill, which overlooks the pellucid waters of the Seekonk River is a rude cell, resides a Hermit, whose history is as inexplicable as his affected account of himself is mysterious. His name is Robert, but to what country he belongs, or what are the inducements which have led him to lead the solitary life of a Hermit, no one knows, and the fact puts conjecture at a hazard. Certain it is, however, that he is not a native of New England; and that he is not by education or by principle attached to our habits or our institutions the whole course of his life, since he has been with us, has abundantly proven.

It is now about eighteen years, since he first visited us, and took up his abode in a thick pine grove, which threw its luxurious foliage over the brow of Arnold's Hill, and from that day to this, he has carefully avoided answering any questions, which might lead to a discovery of his history--or gratify the curiosity of the inquirer.

Months, years and days pass by him unnoticed and unregarded, and it is only on extraordinary occasions, that he emerges from the confines of his solitary hermitage. In the Spring he sometimes occupies himself in laborious employment--such as attending gardens for the neighborhood; but so regardless is he of the things of this world, that he cares not whether his labors are rewarded or not, by those who receive the benefits of them.

Unused to the luxuries or extravagencies of life, he contents himself with the simplest food and such as the bountiful hand of nature supplies. The meats and intemperate liquids of social life, are unknown to him.

> "But from the mountain's grassy side
> A guiltless feast he brings;
> A scrip with herbs and fruits supplied,
> And water from the springs."

In summer, he cultivates a small lot of land, which he is kindly allowed to possess, by the Hon. Mr. BURGES, the owner of the estate on which the hermit is located; but he rarely allows the plants to arrive at maturity, before he plucks them from the earth, and throws them to the cattle that feed around his lonely mansion. What should induce him to thus destroy what he has often been at great labor to cultivate, he assigns no reason, nor can any one form a reasonable conjecture. His cell is decorated with various shells and bones, and is scarcely capable of accommodating himself alone; and the furniture with which it is supplied, consists of a stool, an oaken bench, on which he reposes, and two or three pieces of broken delf ware. It is gloomy, as darkness and solitude can make it, and appears to be admirably fitted for a misanthrope and a recluse.

In winter he seldom emerges from his solitary mansion, but silently and patiently waits for time to introduce the vernal Spring, and to bring about that joyful season, when once more he can rove around the adjacent woodlands and meads. The rays of the sun never enters the portals of his domicil, and at mid-day it assumes all the darkness of midnight. Content with his situation, and at peace with all, he quietly looks forward for the arrival of that day when he shall "bid the waking world good night," and find in countries unexplored, that happiness which life has denied him.

His cell is surrounded by a thick set hedge wrought of wild briars and hemlock, and displays much ingenuity and taste. It is in a most romantic situation, some distance from any human habitation and not often annoyed by the gaze of the curious or the mischievous visits of the boys, for they all love poor ROBERT. It is well worth the trouble for those who are fond of the curious, and are pleased with noticing the excentricities of frail mortality to visit the abode of ' ROBERT THE HERMIT." [* The preceding are the remarks alluded to, contained in the Cadet of 1826, and which we doubt not were from the able pen of the Editor of that paper, at the date mentioned.]

It was not until within a few weeks that the writer was induced to visit the lonely and solitary retreat of "poor Robert,"--by the urgent solicitations of a few who had long known him, and not without hopes that he might possibly be prevailed upon to disclose some of the most extraordinary incidents of his life, for publication, if assured that he was to reap a benefit thereby (for great indeed are his present wants,) the writer was induced to visit him for this purpose. It was about 11 o'clock in the forenoon when I reached his habitation, and on removing a small rough board supported by a leathern hinge, and which closed the only passage to his dark and gloomy cell, I discovered him in about the centre, seated on a wooden block, in an apparent reverie.

I accosted him in a friendly manner, and he with much civility, bid me welcome; and as if willing to permit me to satisfy the curiosity which he no doubt supposed had alone prompted me (as it had hundreds of others) to visit him, he with much apparent good humour invited me to enter, and accept his seat, when, as he observed, I would have a better opportunity to inspect the internal part of his lonely habitation--an invitation which I accepted--and, after making known to him the true object of my visit, and with assurances that it was produced by the most urgent solicitations of one or more of his friends, who had expressed, and I believed sincerely felt an interest in his welfare, so far at least as to render his situation more comfortable--I begged that he would gratify me with a brief narration of his life, and inform me what powerful cause had arose to induce him to quit the pleasures of society, and consign his days to voluntary seclusions?--to which, after a considerable pause, and with his eyes fixed steadfast upon me, as if to satisfy himself that what I had stated was spoken in sincerity, he made the following reply--"that is a relation with which I have declined indulging anyone, as the enquiry seemed merely made to gratify idle curiosity; but, as you speak as if you could feel sympathy for distress, I will briefly gratify your request:--

"I was born in Princeton (New Jersey) in the year 1769 or '70, and was born, as was my mother (who was of African descent,) in bondage; although my father, as has been represented to me, was not only a pure white blooded Englishman, but a gentleman of considerable eminence--I had no brothers and but one sister, who was three years older than myself; but of her, as of my mother, I have but a faint recollection, as I in my infancy was included in the patrimonial portion of my master's oldest daughter, on her marriage to a Mr. *JOHN VOORHIS*, by birth a German. When but four years of age I was conveyed by my master to Georgetown (District of Columbia,) to which place he removed with his family, and never have I since been enabled to learn the fate of my poor mother or sister, whom, it is not very improbable, death has long since removed from their unjust servitude.

At the age of 14 or 15, my master apprenticed me to a Shoemaker, to obtain if possible a knowledge of the art; but making but little proficiency, he again took me upon his plantation, where my time was mostly employed in gardening until about the age of nineteen. It was at that age, that I became first acquainted with an agreeable young female (an orphan) by the name of *ALLEY PENNINGTON*, a native of Cecil county, (Maryland)--she first expressed her attachment to me, and a willingness to become my partner for life, provided I could obtain my freedom, nor can I say that I felt less attachment for one with whom I was confident I could spend my life agreeably-- she was indeed the object of my first love, a love which can only be extinguished with my existence; and never at any period previous was the yoke of bondage more goarding, or did I feel so sensibly the want of that freedom, the deprivation of which, was now the only barrier to my much wished for union with one I so sincerely and tenderly loved.

As my master had uniformly expressed an unwillingness to grant me my freedom, on any other terms than receiving a suitable compensation therefor, my only alternative now to obtain it, was to apply to one with whom I was most intimately acquainted, and to whom I thought I could safely communicate my desires, as he had in more than one instance, expressed *much regard for me, and a willingness to serve me--to him I proposed that he should pay to my master the stipulated sum (Fifty Pounds,) demanded for my freedom, and that the bill of sale should remain in his hands, until such time as I should be enabled by the fruits of my industry to repay him, principal and interest, and allow him suitable compensation therefor for his trouble--to this proposal he readily assented, and not only expressed his willingness but his approbation of my much desired union with my beloved ALLEY. My request was immediately complied with, the Fifty Pounds were paid by my good friend (as I then supposed him,) to whom I was by bond transfered as his lawful property, and by whom I was given to understand that I might then seek business for myself, and turn my attention to any that I should conceive the most profitable, and consider myself under no other bondage than as a debtor, to the amount paid for my freedom. The name of one who had manifested so much what I supposed real and disinterested friendship for me, but who finally proved the author of almost all the wretchedness, which I have since endured, ought not to be concealed--it was JAMES BEVENS.*

Feeling myself now almost a free man, I did not, as may be supposed suffer many hours to elapse before I hastened to bear the joyful tidings of my good fortune, to one, who, as I had anticipated, received it with unfeigned demonstrations of joy; and who, so far from exhibiting an unwillingness to fullfill her promise, yielded her hand without reluctance or distrust--we were married, lawfully married, and more than three years of domestic felicity passed away, without a misfortune to ruffle our repose--in the course of which the Almighty had not only been pleased to bless us with two children, but myself with so great a share of good health, as to have enabled me by my industry, to earn and refund a very considerable portion of the fifty pounds paid by Bevins for my freedom--of these sums I had neither made any charge, or took any receipts--in this I was brought to see my error, but, alas! too late.

Bevins, as I have stated, was a man in whom I had placed implicit confidence, and indeed until the period mentioned, supposed him, as regarded myself, incapable of any thing dishonorable, much less of being the author of as great an act of cruelty and injustice, as ever was recorded in the catalogue of human depravity!

It was late one evening, an evening never to be forgotten by me, while sitting in the midst of my innocent and beloved family, amused with the prattle of my eldest child, and enjoying all the felicity which conjugal love and parental affections are productive of, that this monster in human shape (Bevins) accompanied by another, entered, seized and pinioned me! And gave me to understand that I was intended for a Southern market!! It is impossible for me to describe my feelings or those of my poor distracted wife, at that moment! It was in vain that I intreated, in vain that I represented to Bevins that he had already received a very great proportion of the sum paid for my freedom--to which the ruffian made no other reply, than pronouncing me a liar, dragged me like a felon from my peaceable domicil--from my beloved family--whose shrieks would have pierced the heart of any one but a wretch like himself!

In the most secret manner, at eleven at night, I was hurried on board a Schooner, where additional miseries awaited me!--for fear of an escape, I found irons were to be substituted for the ropes with which they had bound me! And while a person was employed in riveting them, I improved the opportunity, which I though probably would be the last, to address the author of my miseries, in words nearly as follows:--"are these the proofs, master Bevins, of the friendship which you have professed for me! Tell me I pray you, what have I done to merit such barbarous treatment from your hands? Nothing, no nothing! I have nothing wherewith to reproach myself but my own credulity!"--to this he made no reply; shackled and handcuffed, I was precipitated into the hold of the schooner, by the motion of which I perceived was soon under way, and bearing me I knew not whither! So far from feeling any inclination to sleep, it was to me a night of inconceivable wretchedness! I could here nothing but the shrieks of my poor disconsolate wife, and the moans of her helpless children! Indeed such was my imagination--alas! He alone can have a just conception of my feelings who may have been placed in similar situation, if such a person can be found on earth.

In three days (during which no other food was allowed me but a few pounds of mouldy bread) the Schooner reached the port of her destination--Charleston, S. C.--and from which, without being relieved of my irons, I was conveyed to and lodged in prison, where I was suffered to remain in solitude five days-- from thence I was conducted to a place expressly appropriated to the sale of human beings! Where, like the meanest animal of the brute creation, I was disposed of at public auction to the highest bidder.

Resolved on my liberty, and that I would not let pass unimproved the first opportunity that should present, to regain it, I did not remain with my purchaser long enough to learn his name or the price paid for me; who, to win my affections, and the better to reconcile me to my situation, professed much regard for me and made many fair promises (not one of which it is probable he ever intended to perform,) and the better to deceive me, voluntarily granted me the indulgence to walk a few hours unguarded and unattended about the city, without a well authenticated pass--of this I was not ignorant, and therefore sought other and less dangerous means to escape, for I felt that death in its worst forms would be far preferable to slavery.

I carelessly strolled about the wharves among the shipping, where I at length was so fortunate as to find a Sloop bound direct to Philadelphia--she had completed her lading, her sails were loosed and every preparation made to haul immediately into the stream--watching a favourable opportunity, while the hands were employed forward, I unperceived ascended and secreted myself between two casks in the hold--all beneath was soon well secured by the hatches, and I had the satisfaction to find myself in less than three hours, from the time that I was purchased like a bale of goods at auction, stowing snugly away, and with fair prospects of regaining my liberty! It was at that moment that a secret joy diffused itself through my soul--I found unexpected consolation and fortitude, produced by a firm persuasion that by the assistance of a divine providence I should accomplish my deliverance.

Early in the morning of the fourth day from that of our departure, we were safely moored along side of one of the Philadelphia wharves. During the passage of three days and one night, my only nourishment had been about one fill of spirits, contained in a small viol, with which I occasionally moistened my lips, for on the third day my thirst had become intolerable.

I was as fortunate in leaving the sloop unsuspected or discovered, as I had been in secreting myself aboard her, and as soon as safely on shore; my first object was to procure lodgings and something to satisfy the cravings of nature, at a boarding house for seamen. Representing myself as belonging to a coaster, I was not suspected as any other than a free man. As I had heard much of the hospitality of the Quakers (or Friends,) and as a class who were zealous advocated for the emancipation of their fellow beings in bondage, to one of them, on the very day of my arrival, I made my situation known, concealing nothing; and begged that he would interest himself so far in my behalf as to advise me what I had best do, to secure my person from further by unjust claimants, and to restore to me my bereaved and afflicted family.

The good man listened with much apparent attention to my story, and seemed somewhat affected thereby, and so far from exhibiting any disposition to discredit any part of it, presented me with half a crown, and requested me to call on him in the *forenoon of the next day, by which time (as he said) he would have an opportunity to consult some of his brethren, by whom he thought steps would be taken to redress my wrongs--nor have I any reason to believe that he promised more than he intended to perform, and I believe that by these good people I should have been effectually freed from the shackles of slavery, had not another melancholly instance of adverse fortune, placed me in a situation not to comply with his request. Returning to my lodgings in the evening, I was accused (jocosly, as I at first supposed) by the inmates of the house, of being a run-away slave! still however persisting in my former story, that I was free and belonged to a coaster, but being unable to reply satisfactorily to their enquiries, as to the name and place of destination of the vessel, I was committed to prison and advertized as a suspected runaway.*

By what means my pretended master obtained information of my situation, I could never learn, for after nine days close confinement in prison (during which I was not permitted to communicate with any one but the goaler) I was once more strongly ironed and delivered over to the charge of the captain of a Charleston packet--to which port as it proved she was bound direct. It will not be necessary to inform you that my treatment was no better than what I had received on my late passage from Maryland--nor do I know that I could have reasonably expected any better, from those who probably considered coloured people as free from feelings as understandings. As soon as we reached Charleston, I was conducted to and delivered over to my reputed master, who had however in my absence, as it appeared, become somewhat sick of his purchase, for the next day I was with two or three others similarly situated, exposed to sale at public auction.

The person by whom I was next purchased, was a Dr. PETER FERSUE, a man of considerable wealth, and who, had it not been obtained by the toils of his fellow creatures in bondage, might have passed for one not entirely devoid of humanity, for I must say, in justice to him, that it was remarked that those who were held in bondage by him, were treated with less severity than those possessed by some of his neighbors. Perceiving that I was not a little dissatisfied with my situation, and that I possessed a partial knowledge of letters (which I had acquired previous to my marriage) through fear probably that I might instill into the minds of some of my fellow slaves, principles, which might ultimately prove to his disadvantage, I was selected as a house servant, and consequently exempted from many of the privations to which the other slaves were exposed--yet, I became no more reconciled to my situation, nor felt any degree of attachment for him, as I could never harbour a belief but that human beings, whatever might be their complexion were all created equally free; and that it was in direct contradiction to the will of the Supreme Being, that one portion of his creatures should be held in bondage by another, for no other fault than a difference of complexion!--and, I must confess, that my bosom could not but swell with indignation, when placed in a situation to witness the severity with which many of my fellow companions in bondage, at the South, were treated--worn out by constant fatigue, clad in rags, branded with lashes, and otherways treated more like brutes than human beings!

Freedom, the gift of Heaven, was too highly prized by me to permit any thing of less importance to occupy my mind--but, great as were my desires to enjoy it, with him by whom I was wrongfully claimed, I spent eighteen months in servitude, before an opportunity presented to obtain it. The means by which I was finally enabled to effect my escape, were very similar to those which I had practiced in my last attempt--I succeeded in secreting myself in the hold of a brig ready laden, and bound direct to Boston (Massachusetts,) and without an opportunity to provide myself with a drop of water, or a morsel of food of any kind on which to subsist during the passage.

Although the place of my concealment afforded nothing better on which to repose than a water cask, yet I found my birth not so uncomfortable as one would naturally imagine, and I was enabled to endure the calls of hunger and thirst, until the close of the fifth day from that of our departure, when the latter became too oppressive to be longer endure--had I then possessed the wealth of the Indias, it appeared to me, that I should have made a willing exchange for a draught of sweet water; not however until nearly deprived of my senses, did I feel willing to make my situation known to those on board--on the reflection, that should it even cost me my life, that an instantanious death would be preferable to a lingering one, I seized a fragment of a hoop, with which I crawled to and commenced thumping upon a beam near the hatchway, at the same time hallooing as loud as the strength my lungs would admit of--soon I was heard by the hands on deck, and while some broke out in exclamations of wonder and surprize, others ran affrighted to the cabin, to proclaim to the captain the fact that "the brig was most certainly haunted, and had become the habitation of bodiless spirits, as one or more were at that moment crying out lamentably in the hold!"--bodiless spirits they no doubt concluded they must be, for the hatches being so well secured with a tarpolin, none other, as they supposed, could have obtained access.

The captain less superstitiously inclined, ordered the hatches to be immediately raised, but so great a terror of the sailors, that it was sometime before any could be found of sufficient courage to obey.

The hatches were no sooner removed than I presented myself to their view, trembling through fear, pale as death, and with hardly strength sufficient to support myself!--my appearance was indeed such as almost to confirm the superstitious opinion of the sailors, that the brig must certainly be haunted, for in me they beheld, as they supposed, naught but an apparition! The ghost, probably of some unfortunate shipmate, who on a former voyage for some trifling offence, had been privately and wickedly precipitated from the brig's deck into the ocean!--such indeed is the weakness and superstition peculiar to many of that class of people, who follow the seas for a livelihood.

Those on board became however a little less intimidated, when I assured them that I intended them no harm, and was no other than one of the most unfortunate and miserable of human beings, who had sought that means to escape from unjust and cruel bondage! And then briefly related to them, at what time and in what manner I succeeded in secreting myself unnoticed in the brig's hold; where it was my intention to have remained, if possible, until her arrival at the port of her destination--and concluded with begging them for mercy's sake, to grant me a bucket of fresh water for, indeed, such was my thirst, that a less quantity it appeared to me would have proved insufficient to have allayed it.

The captain (who very fortunately for me, proved to be a Quaker, and with all the tender feeling peculiar to that excellent class of people) gave orders to his men to treat me with kindness, and to assist me on deck, for I had now become so weak and emaciated by long fasting, that I was scarcely able to help myself. "Thy wants shall be supplied (said the good captain, addressing himself to me) but such is thy present weakness, that thee must eat and drink sparingly, or it may be worse for thee!"--this man was truly in practice, as well as by profession, a Christian--for had he been my father, he could not have treated me with more tenderness and compassion--he would not allow me but a single gill of water at a draugh, and that quantity but twice in an hour, although five times that quantity would not have satisfied me--and the food allowed me was apportioned accordingly.

In two days after we reached Boston, where I was landed, with permission of the captain to proceed whither I pleased; not however until he had imparted to me some friendly advise, to be cautious with whom I associated on shore, and as I valued my liberty, not to frequent such parts of the town as was inhabited by the most vicious and abandoned of the human race--with which he presented me with some change, and bid me farewell, and never to my knowledge have I since had the happiness to meet with this good man; who, long 'ere this has probably been numbered with the just, and if so, is now I trust reaping the reward of his good deeds in another and better world.

Unacquainted then with the laws of New-England, and fearful that it might not be safe to tarry a long while in a place so populous as Boston, before sunset of the same day I crossed the bridge leading to Charlestown, with an intention of proceeding as far east as Portland--I tarried that night at Lynn, and at about 10 o'clock the next morning reached Salem, where I concluded to remain until the morning ensuing. I applied to a boarding house for seamen for some refreshment, and bespoke lodgings for the night, and in the course of the day met with a gentleman who was in quest of hands for a voyage to India. As my small funds were now nearly exhausted, I thought this not only a favourable opportunity to replenish them, but to place myself beyond the reach of my pretended masters of the south, should they extend their pursuit of me as far east as Massachusetts--to him I therefore offered myself for the voyage, and was accepted.

It cannot be expected that I can recollect, or is it necessary for me to state every minute circumstance that attended me on this voyage, and I will only remark, that although a fresh hand, and totally unacquainted with seamanship, I succeeded in the performance of my duty beyond my expectations, and I believe not only to the satisfaction of my officers, but gained the esteem and good will of my shipmates on board--in proof of this, there is one circumstances that I ought not fail to mention--when about to cross the line, where sailors generally calculate to receive a formal visit from Neptune, the aged Monarch of the deep made his appearance as usual, and with little ceremony introduced himself on board, and while others (who had never before been honored with an interview with his majesty) were *compelled to yield to the unpleasant severities of a custom prescribed by him, I was, by the intercession of my shipmates, so fortunate as to escape.*

After an absence of about fourteen months, the ship returned in safety to Salem, and with the loss I believe of but one man-- when discharge, my wages were punctually paid me, which amounted to a sum not only much greater than what I had ever before been in possession of, but a sum much more considerable than what I once ever expected to possess!--there was indeed as I then thought, but one thing wanting to complete my happiness (to wit.) the presence of my poor unfortunate family!--with this money, thought I, how comfortable could I render the situation of my beloved ALLEY, and my not less beloved children! Who, while I at this moment have enough and to spare, it is not improbable, if living, are enduring all the miseries that poverty and oppression are productive of!--reflections like these were sufficient to depress my spirits, and to deprive me of that enjoyment, which sailors so abundantly participate in on their return from a long voyage to their favorite port.

I remained on shore but a short time when I shipped for a second voyage to India--and, would here briefly state, without entering into particulars, that from this period of nine years, I continued to sail as a common hand from the ports of Boston and Salem, to different ports in Europe and India--in which time I never once suffered shipwreck, or met with any very serious disaster!--it is not improbable that there are at the present day, some of my old Commanders and Shipmates still living in or about Boston and Salem, who may have some recollection of "ROBERT."

After my return from my first voyage, I became acquainted with and commenced board in the family of a respectable widow woman, who afforded decent fare, although in a very moderate circumstances--the family was composed of the old lady and three daughters, of the ages of eighteen, twenty-one and twenty-

five--it was their house that I continued to "hail" as my home, whenever I returned to port, and so long as I remained on shore; and, almost destitute as I was at this time of other friends, it is not, as I deem it, very extraordinary that I should feel more than a common degree of regard and attachment for the family, and that that attachment should finally lead to greater intimacy--this was indeed the case, and on my return from my second voyage, I entered into the bands of matrimony with one of the daughters--the marriage ceremonies were performed by a Justice Putnam, of Danvers. Here, in justification of myself, for having consented to become the husband of another, when there was a possibility of my first wife being alive, I must state that there were two great inducements-- one, that I was strongly urged so to do by those who undoubtedly had the authority to use compulsory means had I declined--and the other, that I had now given up all hopes and expectations of ever meeting again in this world, her, who was the first object of my pledged love.

The day after my marriage I rented a small tenement, which I gave my mother and her daughters liberty to occupy with my wife in my absence, for in three days after I was once more on my favorite element, bound to India--previous to my departure however, I made ample provision for the support of my family, and left a request with the gentleman in whose employ I sailed, to allow them a portion of my wages, in my absence, which was strictly complied with. The voyage proved as usual prosperous, and on my return was received by my friends, not only with the most lively demonstrations of joy, but with the tidings that I had in my absence, for the third time, become a father.

I remained on shore about three months, and such was the harmony that prevailed between us, and such the kind treatment that I received from my companion, that it would have been cruel to have doubted her love and affection for me. At the expiration of the three months, I once more with considerable reluctance bid her adieu, and shipped on board the Herald, capt. DERBY, bound from Boston to Canton;--on this voyage I was absent but about eighteen months, from the time that we left Boston, which was out port of entry on our return.

As soon as discharged I hastened to Salem with the fruits of my toil, and with fond expectations of being welcomed once more to my peaceful home, by one who had so repeatedly expressed her love and regard for me--but, alas, sadly was I disappointed!--for true it is, that she who I had supposed almost an angel in disposition, had in my absence been transformed to a demon! Cold indeed was the reception that I met with--so far from expressing or manifesting the least degree of joy or satisfaction on the occasion (although I had been between one and two years absent) I was insultingly told by her that "if I had never returned she would have been the last to lament it!"

The cause of this surprizing and unexpected alteration in one, whom, from the moment she became my wife, I had treated with so much regard and affection, I was never able to learn-- although I did not and could not feel that ardent affection for her, as for one who was the object of my first love, yet my affection for my child was as great as that for my first born--for this I felt willing to make almost any sacrifice, could a reconciliation have been thereby effected; but it could not, and a final seperation was the consequence. I continued in Salem eight or ten months longer, supporting myself with the fruits of what I obtained by labour on board vessels, on the wharves, &c. and then, with light feet but a heavy heart, started in quest of new friends and a new home, bending my course southerly.

I made no longer tarry on the road than to obtain refreshments, until I reached Providence (Rhode Island) where I made application for, and obtained employment for a few days; at the conclusion of which, I obtained a birth on board of one of the Packets plying between Providence and New-York, in which business I continued (with the exception of a part of the time that I was occasionally employed on shore,) eight or nine years-

-some few of the packet masters with whom I have sailed, some for whom I occasionally wrought on shore, are still living.

Feeling a strong inclination once more to visit the shores of the south, where I had not only been unjustly deprived of my liberty, but where I was inhumanly forced from my beloved wife and two darling children, I took passage (about fifteen years since) on board a sloop for Baltimore, and from thence proceeded direct to Georgetown. As twenty years had elapsed since I there left all that I held most dear in life--and so great a change had time effected in my personal appearance, I felt little or no apprehension that I should be recognized or molested by any, if living, who once professed a claim to me. In this I was not mistaken, for indeed as regarded the town, inhabitants, &c. so great a change had the twenty years produced, that I walked the streets at mid-day unnoticed and unknown. My old master (Voorhis and his wife had been some years dead, and the survivors of the family had removed to parts unknown--Bevins, the wretch by whom I was unjustly deprived of my liberty, and thereby forever seperated from my unfortunate family, had a few years previous emigrated to the west--but, the principle object of my visit was not answered--of my wife and children I could obtain no satisfactory information--all that I could learn, was, that soon after my disappearance, their sufferings and deprivations became so great, that my poor wife in a fit of desparation, as was supposed, put an end to her existence, and that her helpless children did not long survive her!--this was enough! yea more than enough, to fill to the brim the bitter cup of my afflictions!--afflictions which had more less attended me through life!--I then felt but little desire to live, as there was nothing then remaining to attach me to this world--it was at that moment that I formed the determination to retire from it--to become a recluse, and mingle thereafter as little as possible with human society.

With this determination I returned direct to Rhode Island, and soon after selected a retired spot well suited to my purpose, being an extreme point of uninhabited land (Fox Point) situated about one mile south of Providence bridge--there I built me a hut and dwelt peaceably therein for several years, and until annoyed and discommoded by the youth of the town, and by labourers employed in levelling the hill in the neighborhood of my dwelling--I then applied to and obtained the consent of the gentleman (Hon. TRISTAM BRUGISS) to whom the land belongs, to build this hut, and permission to improve the spot of ground enclosed during my life--here in solitude I have dwelt more than six years--once or twice a week (and sometimes oftener) I leave my recess, cross over the bridge into Providence, converse a little with those with whom I have become acquainted, obtain a few necessaries, and return again well satisfied to my peaceable dwelling."

Here Robert concluded his narrative, and which the writer, with very little variation, recorded as he received it from his own lips--in dates, Robert may not have been perfectly correct, as he does not profess to be very positive as to his exact age-- but, in every particular, not a doubt remains on the mind of the writer but that Robert (according to his best recollection) undeviatinglyrelated facts as they occurred--the writer thinks that he may safely draw this conclusion, from the circumstance of having visited him three days successively, and that his replies to the most strict enquiries on the third day, agreed perfectly with the particulars of his narration on the first and second--and as he has heretofore manifested an unwillingness to disclose to any one the secret of his adventures, it is not probable that he formed and committed to memory a story with which to deceive the public, and in which there is not a word of truth--no, those who are best acquainted with "poor artless Robert" know him incapable of such a piece of deception.

ROBERT, is apparently about 60 years of age, a little short of six feet in height, inclined to corpulency, his features perfectly regular, and of complexion but a shade or two darker than that of many who profess to be and pass for whites--in his early years he states that it was much more fair, but of late years have been so much exposed to the smoke of his cell, has become much changed--the lower part of his face is covered with a thick and curly beard, of a jet black, and of uncommon lengths--his garments (or many of them) are of his own manufacture, and whenever a breach appears in any one article, it is either closed by him in a bungling manner, with needle and twin, or a patch is applied without regard to the quality or colour of the cloth. The tattered surtout coat commonly worn by him, in his excursions abroad in winter, in imitation of the military, he has fancifully faced with red, in which (with a cap of the same cloth and with his long beard) it would not be a very surprizing if he should sometimes be viewed by strangers, as some distinguished embassador from the court of Tombuctoo, or one of the loyal subjects of the Grand Seniour, clad in the military costume of his country.

Robert is remarkably abstemious and otherwise correct in his habits--never known to be guilty of profanity--is civil and agreeable in his manners, polite and condescending to all who visit him, and always willing to gratify the curiosity of such as feel disposed to inspect the internal part of his cell--and ever grateful for presents made him. He appears perfectly reconciled to and satisfied with his retired situation, and on the writer's expressing some surprize that he should prefer a secluded life, to that of the enjoyment of society, he observed that he had been too long the subject of the frowns and persecutions of a portion of his fellow beings, to derive that pleasure and satisfaction from their society which the less unfortunate might naturally enjoy.

The walls of his cave or cell, are constructed principally of round stones, of inconsiderable size rudely thrown together, and externally have as much the appearance of being the produce of nature as of art; and although they form a square of thirty or forty feet in circumference, yet are so thick and massy, as to enclose only a single apartment of not sufficient size to contain more than two or three persons at a time, and so low as not to admit of their standing erect, and indeed is in every respect of much less comfortable construction than many of out pig pens!-- about the centre there is a fire place rudely formed, from which proceeds a flue in form of a chimney--and at the extreme end of his cell Robert has constructed a birth or bunk, in which, filled with rags and straw, he reposes at night--beside the fire place stands a block, detached from the butt of an oak, which not only serves him for a seat and table, but being partly hollowed, inverted, for a morter, in which he occasionally pounds his corn, and of which when sufficiently refine, he manufactures his bread--in cooking utensils Robert is quite deficient--the one half of an iron pot is the only article made use of by him, in which he prepares his food--a small piece of iron hoop serves him for a knife, and a few articles of damaged delf ware, and an old sea bucket, for the conveyance of water from a neighboring spring, are nearly the whole contents of his wretched hovel!--the materials of which the roof is constructed, are similar to those which compose the walls of cell; and although of many tons of weight, is altogether supported by a few slender half decayed props, on the strength of which depends the life of poor Robert, should they fail, without the possibility of an escape, his hut would instantaniously become his grave!--It is to obtain for him a more safe and convenient habitation, that has induced the author to issue this work, a great proportion of the profits of which will be devoted to that purpose.

To his gloomy cell there are but one or two apertures or loopholes, for the admission of lights which in winter are completely closed (as is every crack and crevice) with seaweed-- this renders the apartment still more dark and gloomy than it otherwise would be, as when the door is closed to expel the cold, Robert remains within, day and night, in almost total darkness. In summer Robert employs a considerable portion of his time in the cultivation of a small spot of ground, contiguous to his hut, of 7 or 8 rods square, which he has inclosed in an ingenious manner with small twigs and interwoven branches of hemlock and juniper--the soils is so extremely barren and unproductive, that it seldom produces annually more than three or four bushels of potatoes, a peck or two of corn, and a few quarts of beans!--yet with this small crop, Robert is apparently better satisfied and more thankful than many, whose insatiable thirst for worldly gain, leads them, not to an acknowledgment of gratitude due the Supreme Author of all good gifts, nut rather (in imitation of the one of whom we read) to most bitter complaints, that their barns are not of sufficient size to contain their abundant crops!

Having been told that Robert devoted a portion of his time to reading, I offered to present him with a Bible, and some religious Tracts, for which he appeared grateful, but informed me that he was already in possession of both--the gift of a pious lady of Providence--which led me to make some enquiries as regarded his religious sentiment--his opinion of the existence of a Supreme Being--of the immortality of the soul--of future rewards and punishment, &c.--to which he unhesitatingly replied, that he never doubted the existence of a Supreme Being, from whom, although invisible to us, nothing could be concealed, and to whom he believed we were all accountable beings, and would hereafter receive rewards or punishments according to the deeds of the body--from this belief he said he derived great consolation--for, although great had been his trials and troubles in this world, he was not without a hope, that by complying with the terms of the gospel of a blessed Redeemer, he might be permitted in another to participate in those eternal enjoyments which were the promised rewards of the faithful.

Humble and retired as may be the situation of Robert, if such truly are his sentiment, and such his well grounded hopes, altho' his bed may be straw, and his table a block--he must be acknowledged a happy man--and, indeed, infinitely more so than when unjustly held in bondage, and compelled to yield to the commands of a tyrannical task-master--and fortunate no doubt would thousands of his enslaved fellow beings at the south, conceive themselves, if they were privileged like him, to breathe the pure air of freedom, even in an hovel more gloomy and wretched, if possible, than the one which he now claims as his own.

As the narrator has imputed a great portion of his sufferings in early life, to the exercise of what the "Republicans" at the south, denominate a "Constitutional right," (to wit.) that of enslaving a portion of their fellow beings of that persecuted race, who are so unfortunate as to differ with them in the complexion of their skins--the writer begs liberty to make this the subject of his closing remarks.

Our forefathers, persecuted and hunted from their native land, committed themselves to the bosom of the deep, choosing to associate with the monsters of the ocean, and to wander at large amid storms and tempests; rather than sacrifice their religion and liberties to the inquisition of an inexorable tyrant. Guided by heaven to these solitary shores, nature received them with open arms and joyfully pressed them to her rugged breast. By their toils and perseverance, by that virtue derived from pure religion, and that industry inspired by liberty, they rapidly increased to a degree of population and opulence which commanded national respectability--and happy should we be could we here add, that such were the principles that continued not only to govern them to the last, but the generation that succeeded them--But alas! It is truth too firmly established that they, 'ere the elapse of many years, as if forgetful of their own persecutions, become in their turn of the persecutors and oppressors of a portion of their unoffending fellow beings! Kidnapping and consigning to slavery the free-born sons of Africa, soon became a traffic, in which some of almost every state in the union were engaged--and which was attended in many instances with acts of the most cruel barbarity--for no other fault or crime than that of being born black, in an unsuspecting moment they were seized, forced from their own country, conveyed to this, where husbands and wives, parents and children, were seperated with as much unconcern as sheep and lambs by the butcher, and with the same indifference disposed of to the highest bidders!--and in bondage were for the most trivial offences made the subjects of torture and punishments to a degree that would cause humanity to recoil at a bear recital. But to the great honour of the sons of New-England, be it mentioned, that they soon became sensible of the wickedness of this abominable traffic, and a strict prohibition was the consequence--an example of humanity, which was soon followed by the middle states, and in which at the present day we believe slavery has become totally extinct.

But, not so with those who inhabit the southern section of our country, who, governed more by principles of self-interest, than of humanity, at the present day feast upon the fruits of the toils of thousands of their enslaved beings--and by whom in some instances, they are treated with less humanity than what the beasts of the field receive! These (or a portion of them) are those who profess to be the zealous advocates of the "RIGHTS OF MAN!" and the professed admirers of that admirable production of human wisdom, the Declaration of Independence, wherein it is proclaimed that "ALL MEN are born Free and EQUAL!"

"I would not have a slave to till my ground,
To carry me, to fan me while I sleep,
And tremble when I wake, for all the wealth
That sinews, bought and sold, have ever earn'd.
No--dear as freedom is, and in my heart's
Just estimation prized above all price,
I had much rather be myself a slave,
And wear the bonds, than fasten them on him."

The heart would sicken at the recital of the punishments inflicted upon and the extreme sufferings of the unhappy slaves of the south--indeed so goarding is the yoke of bondage, that while some are driven to the desperate act of not only destroying their own lives, but that of their wretched offspring--others seek to obtain their freedom by secreting themselves in thick swamps and marshes; where they remain concealed until they either fall victims to, or are compelled by hunger to return again to their masters, and submit to the punishment which those unfeeling wretches deem the merited reward of their disobedience! A remarkable instance of the latter, occurred in the State of North Carolina about 14 years ago, and although the particulars appeared in many of out prints, at that time, yet as they may have escaped the notice of many of our readers, we thought that it would not be improper to republish them--they are from the pen of a respectable gentleman of Petersburgh, communicated to his friend in New-York.--they follow:

"While I resided in Newbern, N. C. in 1814, being informed that a Negro woman and two small children, had been that day brought in, who had been runaways for several years, I felt a wish to go and see them particularly as there was something curious connected with their history. My friend accompanied me to the jail, for they had been lodged there for safe keeping.--We there learned the particulars of the life which they lived, or rather the miserable existence which they dragged out, during the seven years which they spent in the swamps, in the neighborhood of Newbern.

The owner of this woman, about seven years previously, removed to the western country, and carried with him all his slaves, except this woman and an infant daughter, then in the arms of its mother, who, rather than be separated from he husband, who was owned by another person, timely eloped with her child, and completely avoided the vigilance of her pursuers.

Those who are acquainted with the lower section of that state, well know that it abounds in marshes and fens over frown with weeds, and interspersed, in some places with clumps of pine trees. In one of those dreary retreats this woman found means to conceal herself for the space of seven years: and to find the means also for her subsistence, partly by her own exertions and the assistance of her husband, who would occasionally make her a visit. Living in this situation, she soon had an additional burthen upon her hands by the birth of another child.

The manner in which she concealed herself as well as her children from the discovery was truly singular. By the strictest discipline she prevented them ever crying aloud; she compelled them to stifle their little cries and complaints, though urged to it by pinching hunger, or the severest cold. She prohibited them from speaking louder than a whisper. This may appear strange to relate, but it is certainly true; and as a proof that no deception was used in this case it was satisfactorily ascertained, that after they had remained in town for more than a month, in the company of children who were noisy and clamorous, they were not known in a single instance to raise their voices higher than a soft whispers. At first, it was with great difficulty that they could stand or walk erect, and when they did attempt to walk, it was with a low stoop, the bust inclining forward, and with a hasty step like a patridge. But their favorite position was that of squatting upon their hams. In this posture, they could remain for hours without any apparent weariness, and at a given signal would move one after the other with great facility, and at the same time with so much caution, that not the least noise would be heard by their footsteps.

Their method of subsistence was the most extraordinary; sometimes the husband, according to the woman's account would fail to bring them supplies; and whether the fear of detection prevented her from intruding on the rights of others, or whether she was prevented by conscientious motives is not for me to determine--but in this dreadful exigence, she would, for the support of herself and children, have recourse to expedients which nothing but the most pressing necessity could ever suggest.

Frogs and terrapins were considered as rare dainties, and even snakes would be taken as a lawful prize to satisfy the call of hunger.--It was the custom, said the woman in the little family, when they made up a fire in the night, and this was done only in the cold nights of winter, for one to sit up while the others slept. The one who watched had a double duty to perform--not only to do the ordinary duty of a centinel, but to watch for mice; which they contrived in the following manner. The person watching would spread a little meat on the ground, or a few grains of corn or peas, or for want of these, a crust of bread when they had it; over which an old handkerchief or piece of cloth, was spread, then observing a profound and death-like silence, the mice would creep from their retreats in order to possess themselves of the bait.--The centinel, true to his post, as soon as the cloth was moved by the vagrant mouse, would very dexteriously smack down a pair of hands upon him, and secure him for purposes yet to be mentioned. The flesh, as may be supposed, was used for food, which they devoured with as little ceremony as a boy would eat a snow bird; but even the skin was not thrown away: for they being carefully preserved, the hair or fur was picked off, and mixed with wool or cotton for the purpose of making gloves and stockings--and they managed to spin up the materials they could procure, by means of a stick, about six or eight inches in length.-This was held in the left hand, while, with the right, they held the materials to be spun, they gave us a specimen of their adroitness in this art; and the little boy, who was not above five years old, could manage his stick with surprising dexterity.--Several pair of stockings and gloves were shown, which had been knit by these singular beings, during their voluntary banishment.--They were grotesque enough in their appearance, and were made up of a greater medly of materials than are generally used in the civilized world.

How much longer this deluded African, with her two wretched children would have remained in the comfortless savannahs of North Carolina is not known, had not the woman been deserted by her husband.--Being deprived of the solace she derived from his transient visits, and the scanty subsistence she received from his hand, her situation became miserable beyond description. At length emaciated with hunger she crept to the road, gave herself up with her equally meagre looking charge, to the first person she saw, who happened very fortunately to be a man, with his cart going towards town--the sight indeed to the citizen, was a novel one, if we may judge from the number who crowded to see and determine for themselves.'

41269117R10022

Made in the USA
San Bernardino, CA
01 July 2019